EDWARD ELGAR

Five Unaccompanied Part Songs
Opus 71, 72 & 73

for unaccompanied SATB (with divisions)

NOVELLO

Published in Great Britain by Novello Publishing Limited

Exclusive distributors: Hal Leonard
7777 West Bluemound Road, Milwaukee, WI 53213
Email: info@halleonard.com

Hal Leonard Europe Limited
42 Wigmore Street Marylebone, London, WIU 2 RY
Email: info@halleonardeurope.com

Hal Leonard Australia Pty. Ltd. 4
Lentara Court Cheltenham, Victoria 9132, Australia
Email: info@halleonard.com.au

Order No. NOV72325R

www.halleonard.com

Preface

Elgar inherited a love of books from his mother; his library was so extensive as to prompt a contemporary to note that 'no living composer is more widely read than Elgar ... books are his greatest treasure'. So when W.G. McNaught, Novello's choral adviser at the time, suggested to the composer in 1914 that a group of part songs would be eagerly taken up by choirs countrywide, Elgar had a store of possible texts already at hand, first selecting two poems by the seventeenth-century Welsh poet, Henry Vaughan.

For the first setting, Elgar chose the final stanza of Vaughan's *The Shower*. This begins with the word 'Yet', following on from the previous verses, and so Elgar appropriately changed it to 'Cloud'. At the repetition of the opening lines a greater emotional intensity is achieved by a richer spacing of the opening chord in bar 9. Unusually for Elgar this setting is mainly chordal, perhaps in order to throw into relief the patter of raindrops suggested by the middle voices' semiquavers in bar 12. The second Vaughan setting, *The Fountain*, is more complex, with frequent division of parts and ending, rather surprisingly, with the major third supplied by only half of the tenor section in their weakest register.

The other three settings are of Russian poems, translated and adapted by Rosa Newmarch – an accomplished musician and writer of programme notes in the early years of the twentieth century – who had studied in Russia and published translations and adaptations of Russian poetry. These texts seem to have drawn out the best of Elgar. *Death on the Hills* achieves a dramatic power that reaches almost orchestral proportions and represents an aspect of the composer's personality that rarely surfaces. When the poet asks whether it is the wind and rain that darkens the hill slopes, the reply is ''Tis Death who rides across the hills'; the contrast of tone which Elgar demands (compare bars 34 and 44) produces an eerie atmosphere far from the composer's habitual emotional world. He was well aware of his achievement, writing to a friend 'It is one of the biggest things I have done'. He also wrote to Ivor Atkins in Worcester, 'It is, I declare, courageous of you to frighten your people into singing *Death on the Hills*'. It was dedicated to Frances Colvin, wife of Sir Sidney Colvin, Director of the Fitzwilliam Museum, who tried without success to set up an operatic collaboration between Elgar and such writers as Thomas Hardy. It must remain a matter of regret that none of these operatic projects was realised; *Love's Tempest* offers further proof of a sure-footed dramatic instinct. Divisi part writing in the opening adagio gives way to strong unisons and octave doublings in the contrasting sections. Elgar wrote to McNaught concerning the repetition of the word 'roaring': 'Will it give them more chance to breathe and roar more lustily?'

The textures of *Serenade*[1] are fundamentally orchestral rather than vocal, the opening bars suggesting pizzicato strings or gentle woodwinds, with a legato violin theme overlaid at bar 6. The *più mosso* section further suggests a full but *ppp* orchestral tutti.

Appended to three of these part songs are the names of districts of London at that time still predominantly rural. The Elgars had moved from the West Country to Hampstead in 1912 and, to escape the metropolis, would go on motoring tours. In her diary, Alice Elgar noted visits to Mill Hill, Totteridge and Hadley Green with comments on her husband's nostalgia for his native Worcestershire countryside.

Elgar was notoriously volatile in temperament, but friendships once forged were not forgotten and, in a class conscious society, the dedicatees of these songs range far and wide. If Lady Colvin was a society figure, Miss Frances Smart was not. She had been a neighbour in Malvern. Sanford Terry, a renowned Bach scholar, was Professor of History at Aberdeen University, and had set in motion the award of a doctorate to Elgar in 1906. Perhaps the clearest sign of the value the composer placed on his roots was the name of W. Mann Dyson. He was a cathedral lay clerk in Worcester who had grown up with Elgar.

ERIC WETHERELL

---

[1]This poem is by Minsky (the pen name of Nikolai Vilenkin), and not Maikov, as wrongly attributed in the previous Novello edition of these songs.

THE SHOWER

Text
Henry Vaughan

EDWARD ELGAR
(Op. 71, No. 1)

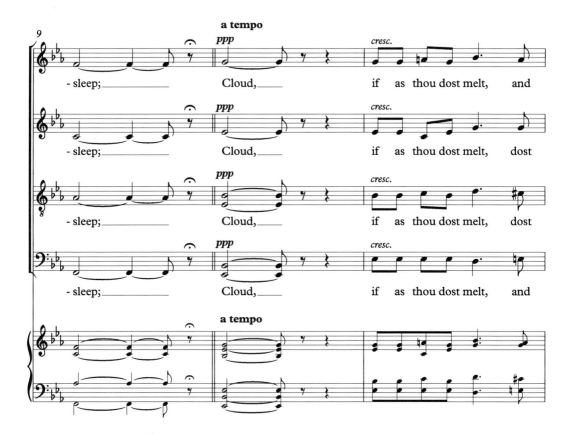

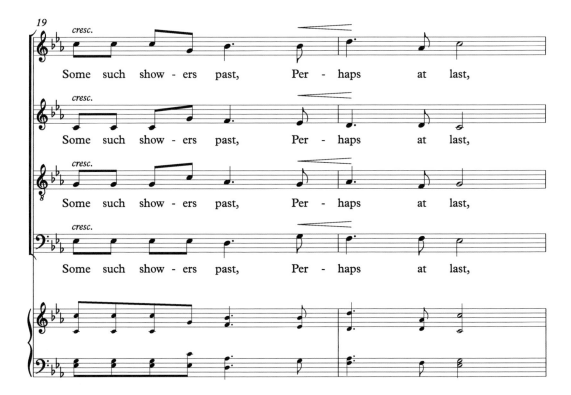

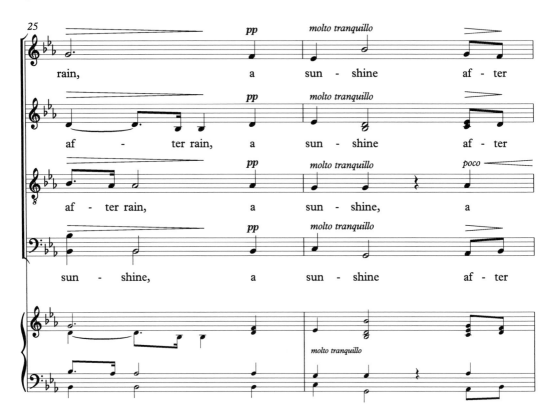

(Mill Hill)

To my friend W. Mann Dyson, Worcester

THE FOUNTAIN

Text
Henry Vaughan

EDWARD ELGAR
(Op. 71, No. 2)

did un-fold Che-quer'd with snow - y fleec - -

and heav'n its a - zure did un - fold Che-quer'd with snow - y

heav'n its a - zure did un - fold, its a - zure Che-quer'd with snow - y

did un - fold___ Che-quer'd with snow - y fleec - -

rall. accel. . . . . . al . . . Tempo 1

- es; The air was all in spice, was all in

fleec - es; The air was all in spice,___ the air was

fleec - es; The air was all in spice, the air was

- es; The air was all in spice, the air was

rall. accel. . . . . . al . . . Tempo 1

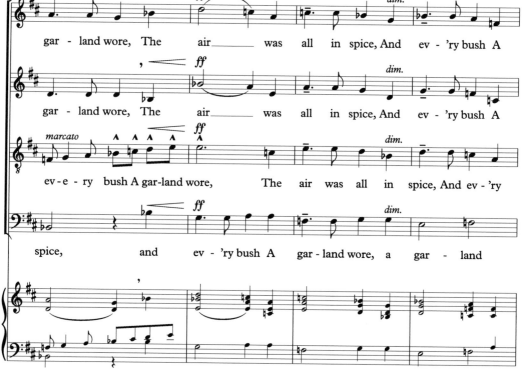

Tempo 1

gar - land wore: thus fed my eyes, But

gar - land wore: thus fed my eyes, But

bush A gar - land wore: thus fed my eyes, But

wore:_____ thus fed my eyes, But

Tempo 1

all the earth lay hush, Thus fed my eyes, But

all the earth lay hush, Thus fed my eyes, But

all the earth lay hush, Thus fed my eyes, But

all the earth lay hush, Thus fed my eyes, thus

(*Totteridge*)

To Lady Colvin

DEATH ON THE HILLS

Text
Rosa Newmarch
adapted from
Maikov

EDWARD ELGAR
(Op. 72)

rain-storms lash and leap?___ No wind blows chill up - on___ them, Nor

rain-storms lash and leap?___ No wind blows chill up - on___ them, Nor

No wind blows chill up - on___ them, Nor

No wind_____ blows, Nor

are they lash'd by rain:___ 'Tis Death who rides a - cross the hills With

are they lash'd by rain:___ 'Tis Death who rides a - cross the hills With

are they lash'd by rain:___ 'Tis Death who rides a - cross the hills With

are they lash'd by rain:___ 'Tis Death who rides a - cross the hills With

- es, The old folk plead with Death:

- es, The old folk plead with Death:

Poco più lento ♩ = 66

(Soprano, Alto and Tenor to be sung with a thin and somewhat veiled tone.)

"O let us take the vil - lage - road, Or by the brook draw breath.

"O let us take the vil - lage - road, Or by the brook draw breath.

"O let us take the vil - lage - road, Or by the brook draw breath.

Poco più lento ♩ = 66

* Only light voices should sing from here to the end; the heavy Tenors may assist the Basses later.

24

* The S.A.T. to be subdued to the end but sung with firm, sobbing accents, and great expression.

48
let us take the vil-lage-road, O let us take the vil-lage-road,
p pp p
O let us take the vil-lage-road, Or by the brook draw breath; There let the old drink wa-ter,
let us take the vil-lage-road, O let us take the vil-lage-road,
p pp p
O let us take the vil-lage-road, Or by the brook draw breath; There let the old drink wa-ter,
let us take the vil-lage-road, O let us take the vil-lage-road,
p pp p
O let us take the vil-lage-road, Or by the brook draw breath; There let the old drink wa-ter,
p
rill, For there the wives and mo - thers all Their
51
There let the old drink wa - ter, There let the
pp
And let the lit - tle chil - dren run And pluck the blos - soms gay;
There let the old drink wa - ter, There let the
pp
And let the lit - tle chil - dren run And pluck the blos - soms gay;
There let the old drink wa - ter, There let the
pp
And let the lit - tle chil - dren run And pluck the blos - soms gay;
cresc.
buck - ets take to fill. The

p

young folk play,_ there let the young folk play,

pp

There let the old drink wa-ter, O let us take the vil-lage-road, O

p

young folk play,_ there let the young folk play,

pp

There let the old drink wa-ter, O let us take the vil-lage-road, O

p

young folk play,_ there let the young folk play,

pp

There let the old drink wa-ter, O let us take the vil-lage-road, O

f

wife might see her hus - band,_ The mo - ther see her

56

pp

O let us take the vil - lage - road, Or by the brook draw breath;

pp

let us take the vil - lage - road, O let_ us

pp

O let us take the vil - lage - road, Or by the brook draw breath;

pp

let us take the vil - lage - road, O let_ us

pp

O let us take the vil - lage - road, Or by the brook draw breath;

pp

let us take the vil - lage - road, O let_ us

sf *p*

son;_ So close they'd cling their

To my friend C. Sanford Terry, M.A., Aberdeen

LOVE'S TEMPEST

Text
Rosa Newmarch
adapted from
Maikov

EDWARD ELGAR
(Op. 73, No. 1)

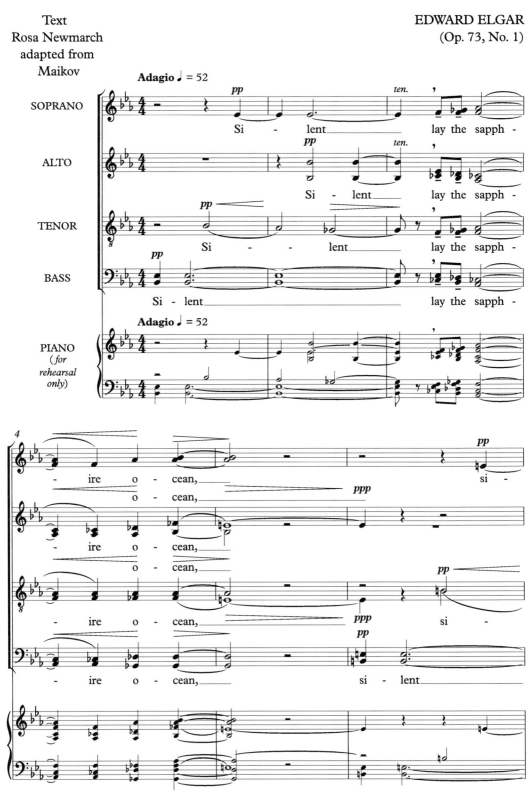

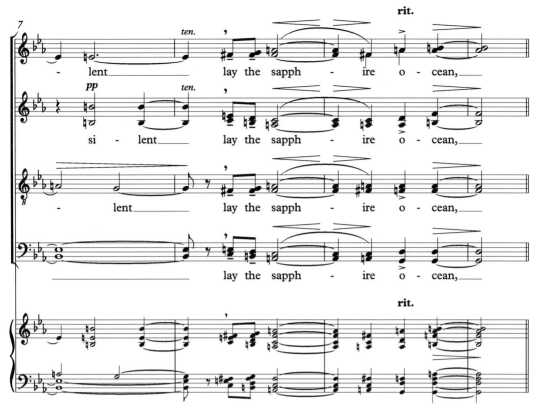

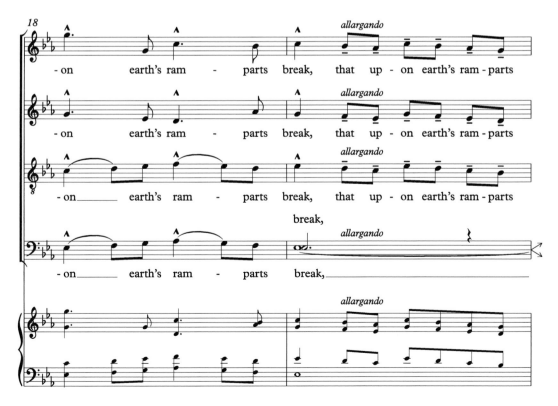

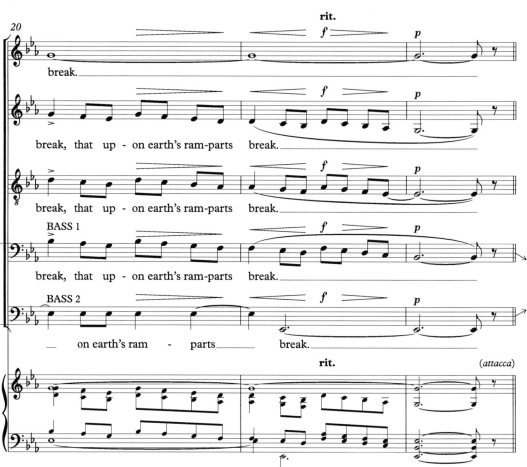

34

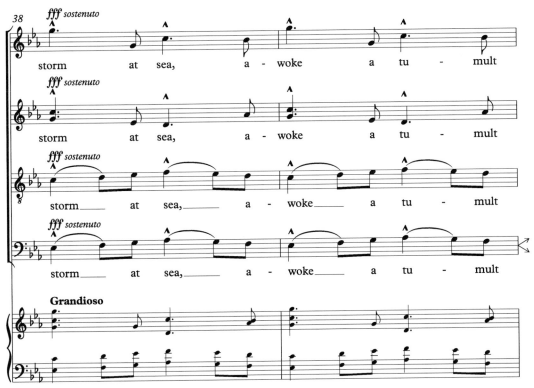

To my friend Percy C. Hull, Hereford

SERENADE

EDWARD ELGAR
(Op. 73, No. 2)

Text
Rosa Newmarch
adapted from
Minsky

May be sung a semitone higher.

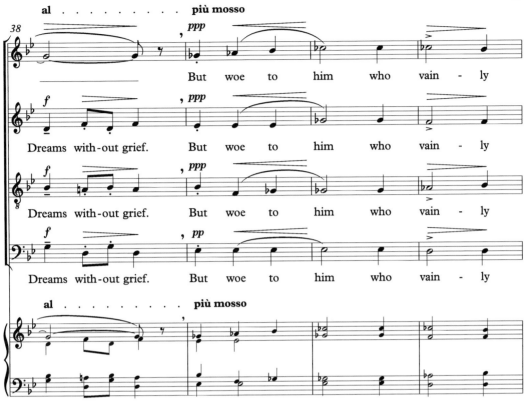

al . . . . **più mosso**

38

ppp

But woe to him who vain - ly

f *ppp*

Dreams with-out grief. But woe to him who vain - ly

f *ppp*

Dreams with-out grief. But woe to him who vain - ly

f *pp*

Dreams with-out grief. But woe to him who vain - ly

al . . . . **più mosso**

molto allargando

42

cresc. molto

calls Through sleep - less nights for ease from

cresc. molto

calls Through sleep - less nights for ease from

cresc. molto

calls Through sleep - less nights for ease from

cresc. molto

calls Through sleep - less nights for ease from

molto allargando

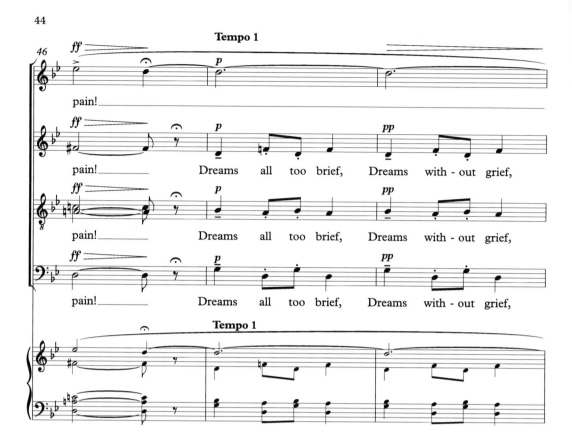

(*Hadley Green*, 1914)